HUSBAND'S EDITION

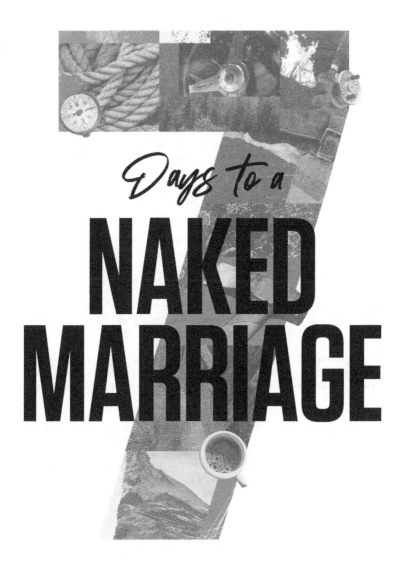

Days to a
NAKED
MARRIAGE

DAVE & ASHLEY WILLIS

CONTENTS

INTRODUCTION

During our premarital counseling, our pastor opened his Bible and read this verse: *"A person standing alone can be attacked and defeated, but two can stand back-to-back and conquer. Three are even better, for a triple-braided cord is not easily broken"* (Ecclesiastes 4:12, NLT). Until that moment, we honestly never thought much about this verse, but after one of our sessions, our pastor gave us a rather unusual wedding gift. He handed us a real triple-braided cord.

He then explained that the verse illustrated a strong marriage in which the husband, wife, and God each represent a strand of the cord, with God being the heartiest strand. This kind of cord is hard to break and extremely secure, but the cord is only as strong as each strand. If one strand is weakened or cut off, the cord loses some of its strength. With enough weight it will eventually fray or break down completely.

The longer we are married and work with married couples, the more we see the truth of this verse played out. We are not sure where you might be in your faith, but we encourage you to keep God at the center of your marriage. So, how do we keep God as the primary strand in our marriage? We do this by making our personal relationship with Christ a priority. We strive to know Him more by going to church and reading our Bibles, and we make prayer a consistent part of our daily lives. When we keep our relationship with God as our top priority, our minds and hearts are more prepared to approach our spouse with the love and devotion he or she deserves, and we essentially keep our strands connected to the master strand. When this happens, our cords of marriage remain strong.

God painted this picture in the very first marriage He created between two human beings—the marriage of Adam and Eve. In

Genesis 2, we learn that God created Adam and then Eve. They were unified with God—like that cord of three strands—and they were also "naked and unashamed." When God created this *naked marriage*, He was revealing to us something more than just sexual intimacy; He was showing the importance of having **complete transparency, vulnerability, acceptance, and intimacy at every level of the relationship**. We're certainly not advocating that we all walk around naked all day (although we do think most marriages would benefit from more naked-time), but we are suggesting that we all need to become more intentional about reconnecting with the true intimacy Adam and Eve got a taste of in the Garden of Eden. Love, in marriage, has to be completely open, honest, and transparent. Secrets are as dangerous as lies and can rob your relationship of intimacy and trust. Love, by its very nature, is honest, and this is especially important to the sacred bond of trust in marriage.

Through our years together and the different seasons of our marriage and family, our love has grown deeper and richer. We've also gained a fuller understanding of what marriage really means. It's not something that can be defined by feelings or captured by words alone. God created marriage to be a transformative force in every aspect of our lives, and once we understand and embrace it, our marriage will come into clearer focus and will grow in deeper levels of intimacy, and vulnerability.

It is our hope and prayer you and your spouse experience this same growing intimacy and vulnerability. Better yet, God *desires* it for you. That's the heart of what a "naked marriage" is all about. Our podcast and our most popular book are both called *The Naked Marriage* because we believe every couple is meant to experience the physical, emotional, and spiritual intimacy Adam and Eve experienced in the Garden of Eden before sin entered the picture. The first couple's nakedness was a picture of God's design for a marriage without secrets, masks, or barriers between a husband and wife. That's still God's plan for marriage today. That's His plan for you.

In this devotional addition to our original *Naked Marriage* book and podcast, we've taken the principles, Scriptures, and stories we've shared in the past and reimagined them in a new format. We've also built on a previous book series called *7 Days to a Stronger Marriage*, which unpacked the marriage vows as the foundation for a strong, life-long relationship. This new devotional series takes the best of what we've shared in these previous books plus some brand-new content to help you build on your marriage vows to live in a vibrant, transparent, passionate, *naked marriage.*

We believe this seven-day journey could become one of the most significant weeks in the history of your love story. It could also be a mountaintop moment in your walk with Jesus Christ. We are praying for you and your spouse as you begin the journey. If you'll give this week your full effort, we believe these next seven days could have a permanent impact on your marriage!

HOW IT WORKS

This book contains seven chapters that are meant to be read one chapter per day over the course of the next seven days. Each chapter takes one specific promise from the traditional marriage vows and explores its meaning and implications in detail. After the daily reading, there will be an activity assignment for you to do based on the reading, along with a journaling section where you can record your thoughts, prayers, and new ideas throughout the process. The final activity at the end of Day Seven will incorporate each of the vows and give you a creative way to renew your vows to your wife.

There are no specific "rules" for what this experience has to look like for you and your wife because we want you to have the freedom and creativity to customize the seven-day experience however works best for you. To get the most out it, we suggest prioritizing daily time to finish the day's reading and taking time to do each day's activity. Then we hope you'll make two different commitments. First, commit to praying for your marriage each day. Then, commit to being encouraging, to giving your best effort, and to approach the process without criticism.

We challenge you to commit to one week in which you can complete the experience with your wife. But even if it takes you seven weeks instead of seven days, the main objective is that you finish this journey and create ongoing new, healthy habits in your marriage.

This journey is meant to be taken in partnership with your wife. Hopefully, she already has the *"Wife's Edition"* of this book, and she's excited to take this journey with you. While it's our hope that couples approach this challenge with equal enthusiasm, we know that in many cases, a husband might be doing this challenge without the full partnership of his wife (or vice versa). Both the male and female versions of this book contain mostly the same content, so you'll both be able to discuss the same stories. However, you can also look forward to some unique content written specifically to a wife and specifically to a husband.

Some of you may be taking this challenge to invest in your marriage, but you feel like you're in it alone. Please don't lose hope! These readings and activities can make an impact on your marriage, and a positive impression on your wife even if she is not currently participating. Your efforts might eventually inspire her to take the challenge with you.

As you start this journey, know that you are pursuing something well worth the time and energy you're going to invest in. Any investment in your marriage is always an investment worth making! We are praying for you and cheering you on in the days ahead. Please feel free to contact us to let us know how the experience is going and how we can encourage you.

Thanks and God bless,
Dave and Ashley Willis
www.DaveAndAshleyWillis.com

Day 1

I TAKE YOU TO BE MY WIFE

EPHESIANS 5:21-23

I remember it like it was yesterday...

I had just returned home for a summer working at camp before my senior year of college. Ashley and I had been talking about marriage since our third date, and the time had come to get the ring and plan a perfect evening. I wanted to close the deal fast before she realized that she was way out of my league and could probably find a much better guy if she looked around!

With the help of her parents, I planned an elaborate story to give me an excuse to go and do some prep work. I told her that I needed to go visit my brother who had just broken his collarbone. I hadn't thought through my backstory well because she said she wanted to come with me, so in a panic, I blurted out, *"You can't...he's naked!"*

"What? Why is he naked?"

"I don't know. When he's injured, he likes to be naked. I know, it's weird, but you can't come. He wouldn't want you to see him like that."

She was disappointed and confused when I left. I had knots in my stomach from nervousness and the guilt of having just told her a ridiculous lie. To this day, I'm terrible at lying to her, which has actually worked out great for our marriage.

I finally made it back to take her to dinner, and everything was ready to go. She looked absolutely stunning in a red dress that brought out the beautiful tones of her strawberry blonde hair. I kept thinking, *"No way is she going to say, 'yes.' She is way out of my league!"*

We went out to the nicest restaurant in town, and I paid a small fortune for a meal I was too nervous to eat. We finally made it to the spot where I planned to pop the question. It was a place called Ashland, which is the estate of the famous Kentucky statesman, Henry Clay. The weather and scenery were beautiful.

My hands were shaking as I pulled out a handwritten letter and began reading it to her. I professed my undying love and commitment. I promised to always love and cherish her and to build our future on a foundation of faith in God. I got down on one knee and asked her to spend her life with me, and she took a deep breath and exclaimed, *"No way!"*

My heart sank until I realized that it was a good "no way." She hugged me and said, "Yes!" That began a journey that led us to a beautiful wedding day where we exchanged those timeless vows, beginning with this promise:

"I, Dave, take you, Ashley, to be my wife."

"I, Ashley, take you, Dave, to be my husband."

Our journey has been a beautiful one since the day we exchanged those vows, but we've come to discover that being a husband and being a wife is more complex than we first realized. While we both had a desire to become a "perfect" spouse, we soon discovered that God's definition of a healthy marriage is often different from what we see in the world around us.

A *Naked Marriage* Requires Vulnerability

When we refer to a "naked marriage," we're not just talking about physical nakedness. Nakedness is also a picture of transparency and vulnerability. When you and your wife exchanged vows on your wedding day, you were promising a lifetime of intimate vulnerability with each other.

The more you love someone, the greater access they have to your heart, and therefore, the greater their potential to hurt you. This can be scary! However, until your vulnerability gives a person the ability to hurt you, you'll never be able to truly experience a beautifully intimate and committed relationship with that person. This reality keeps some people from wholeheartedly committing to and embracing marriage because they're trying to protect their hearts from being wounded again. But if we're not careful, our wounds from the past will create new wounds in our marriage—perpetuating pain and distance in our relationship—until we become intentional about healing from the past and moving forward in a healthy way. As we have interacted with people who have experienced childhood abuse, marital infidelity, or any form of pain and disappointment from the past, we've noticed that many have developed a defense mechanism we call "emotional sunburn."

Ashley

Have you ever gone to the beach and forgotten to apply sunscreen? We used to live in Florida, and this would happen to Dave all the time. He'd think it wasn't a big deal because he'd only be exposed to the sun for a short time, but hours later, his unprotected skin would be lobster red. He would quickly put on a T-shirt to cover up, but without fail, someone in the family would give him a slap on the back or an aggressive hug, and he'd scream in pain.

It felt like he was screaming at us in anger, but he wasn't. It wasn't about us at all. He was sunburned and hurting. We just happened to touch him before he had time to heal.

Dave

So many of us have this emotional sunburn—an invisible burn deep within our hearts and souls, maybe because of things that have happened to us or because of things that we have done. And our wife, due to her proximity to us, will sometimes touch us where we are already wounded, and we'll get angry. Therefore, we need to create an environment in our marriage filled with love and patience. Instead of picking at our wife's burns, we need to be rubbing aloe on her scars—creating a safe place for her to heal. We need to pray for her and ask God to heal her heart. He is the ultimate healer.

Sadly, many of us have an emotional sunburn from being burned in our past. These old scars or wounds, if left untreated, can make us overreact in unhealthy ways toward our loved ones. We push others away to protect ourselves. Whatever you may have done or whatever may have wounded you in the past, healing is possible. God wants you to experience vulnerability and love with your spouse. He wants you to experience a rich, meaningful marriage. He wants to bring you to a place of healing, so you can experience a loving marriage in its fullness.

This kind of trust and vulnerability is only made possible when we practice what the Bible calls "mutual submission." It's a mindset and humble attitude that submits to Christ in all things as we serve our wife's needs in marriage. This concept is introduced in Ephesians 5:21–33. Paul writes:

> "Submit to one another out of reverence for Christ. Wives, submit yourselves to your own husbands as you do to the Lord. For the husband is the head of the wife as Christ is the head of the church, his body, of which he is the Savior. Now as the church submits to Christ, so also wives should submit to their husbands in everything. Husbands, love your wives, just as Christ loved the church and gave himself up for her to make her holy, cleansing her by the washing with water through the word, and to present her to himself as a radiant church, without stain or wrinkle or any other blemish, but holy and blameless. In this same way, husbands ought to love their wives as their own bodies. He who loves his wife loves himself. After all, no one ever hated their own body, but they feed and care for their body, just as Christ does the church—for we are members of his body. "For this reason a

man will leave his father and mother and be united to his wife, and the two will become one flesh." This is a profound mystery— but I am talking about Christ and the church. However, each one of you also must love his wife as he loves himself, and the wife must respect her husband."

It's interesting that Paul first encourages married couples to "submit to one another out of reverence for Christ" before he goes into the specifics of submission (love and respect) for both husbands and wives. And when we read further into these verses, husbands are called to be willing to lay down their lives for their wives, just as Jesus willingly laid down His life for us. Wow! That is a high standard! It even goes on to say that husbands should care for their wives as they care for their own bodies, and as Christ cares for the Church.

As a husband, it's your job to lead. But as Jesus teaches, true leadership is displayed through service and self-sacrifice. As a husband, I remind myself daily that it's not my job to be the "boss" of the house. It's my job to lead my family into a closer walk with Jesus. If I'm not following Him, then I'm headed in the wrong direction. If I'm not leading with love like Jesus does, then I'm not leading at all.

A healthy marriage should never be about leveraging power or control over each other. God created a wife to serve her husband and a husband to serve his wife, as both spouses serve Christ in partnership. You and your wife are a team. Work together to create wholehearted intimacy, vulnerability, and trust. Work together to create the naked marriage God wants you to have.

Living Out the First Promise: "I Take You to Be My Wife."

As you live out this first promise, remember that your vow means you are choosing each and every day to honor your wife over anyone else. You are waking each morning with a renewed commitment to be her best and most loyal friend. You are agreeing to fulfill your unique, God-given role as a husband to the very best of your abilities. You are acknowledging that it is never your responsibility to point out all the ways your wife may be falling short. Support her, pray for her, and encourage her so that you both may become the best spouse that you can be.

PRAYER FOR TODAY

Lord, thank you for my wife. Help me to be the husband she deserves. Help me to love her as you, Jesus, love your own bride, the Church. Help me be a blessing to her and not a burden. Guide me as I serve, lead, and provide for my family's needs. Please make me into the man I was created to be. Thank You for loving me. Thank You for my marriage. Please draw me closer to You and closer to my wife every day.

In Jesus' name,
Amen

FOR JOURNALING AND REFLECTION

- What did I learn about my spouse today?
- What did I learn about myself today?
- What did I learn about the promise, "I take you to be my wife"?
- As a result of what I've learned, I will…

DAY ONE ACTIVITY: REMEMBER YOUR ROOTS

Part of building a great future as husband and wife is rooted in celebrating the past. Tonight, carve out at least thirty minutes to look at old pictures together. Get out your wedding photos or video. Look at old pictures on social media of your family and your early day as a couple. Reminisce about the good times and God's faithfulness during the hard times. Laugh together. Dream about the future together. Being intentional about sharing moments like this will do wonders to keep your marriage united.

_____

_____

_____

_____

_____

_____

_____

_____

_____

_____

_____

_____

_____

_____

_____

_____

_____

_____

_____

_____

_____

_____

_____

_____

_____

_____

_____

_____

_____

_____

_____

_____

_____

_____

_____

_____

_____

_____

_____

_____

_____

_____

_____

_____

_____

_____

_____

_____

_____

_____

_____

_____

_____

_____

_____

_____

_____

_____

_____

_____

_____

_____

_____

_____

_____

_____

_____

Day 2

TO LOVE AND TO CHERISH

---

1 CORINTHIANS 13:4-7

Of all human relationships, God designed marriage to be the most powerful and intimate expression of unity and love. Genesis 2:18 reads, "Then the Lord God said, 'It is not good for the man to be alone. I will make a helper who is just right for him'" (NLT). Next to God's grace, your wife is the most sacred gift God has ever entrusted to you, and you should treat her like the treasure she is. God wants you to be completely unified to your wife in love.

The best way I can describe unity in marriage is through what I call the loveseat principle. To give you an idea of what this looks like, I want you to visualize a loveseat with two individual chairs next to it, just like in most living rooms. These pieces of furniture represent a few different "postures" or relational dynamics that a marriage can have. The first posture is a husband and wife who choose to approach life from the loveseat. Imagine them sitting side by side. They are unified. They're serving each other, communicating openly and honestly, and completely connected. When problems arise, they choose to face them together and work through it.

The second posture is a husband and wife who choose to approach life from the individual chairs or *single* seats. Imagine the space between these chairs. Now, picture these chairs on wheels, slowly moving further and further apart. Those in the single seats are focused on their own needs and likely to blame each other for the marriage not being what they think it should be. When hard times come, they tell themselves they should just call it quits because they are better off alone anyway. We call these the *me seats*.

The third posture is the loneliest one. This occurs when one spouse chooses to approach life from the *loveseat* while the other spouse sits in the *single seat*. The spouse in the *loveseat* wants the marriage to work. They are praying and doing everything they can to fight for their marriage. But, sadly, they are the only one fighting for it. The spouse in the me seat has stopped making their marriage a priority. They don't want to work through it because of their pride and preferences. This is a frustrating and hurtful position to be in, but the good news is that, with God, there is always hope. He can help those in the *single seats* stand up and join each other in the *loveseat*. He softens hardened hearts and brings dead things—even lifeless, out-of-sync marriages—back to life!

Ashley and I believe that every marriage is in one of these three postures, and it is our hope and prayer that all married couples come back together to that *loveseat* and cultivate a unified marriage. We want couples to come to the place where they can say, "It's not all about me and my own needs. I want to serve you, even when I don't feel like it and even when these gestures of goodwill aren't necessarily reciprocated. I want to serve you and give you my best even when you are not in a position to give back. I don't want to treat you the way you may be treating me. I want to treat you the way God treats me. God gives me His best, even when I'm at my worst. And I want to strive to do the same for you."

Friends, God calls us to love each other the way He loves us. And the happiest marriages have a husband and a wife who both understand this principle and do their best to live it out. One way we can live out this principle is by starting each day by asking our spouse, "How can I help you today?" When both husband and wife make it their mission to serve one another, their hearts are going to be filled up in the process, and their marriage will thrive. When a couple takes on this mindset—which goes against our selfish nature—real and lasting transformation happens. The marriage will be happier and healthier.

Now, just because you are in the *loveseat* doesn't mean that you aren't going to have disagreements. It's just that, when you are in that love-seat, you are going to handle disagreements in a healthier way, talking through them until you both reach a resolution. But if both of you are separated in those *single seats*, you are only thinking about your own feelings and your own "rights." When you and your spouse aren't unified, you won't handle the disagreements well. Unity doesn't mean uniformity. A husband and wife certainly won't always see eye to eye. But when you both choose to approach life from the *loveseat*, you consciously choose to face your struggles together—to talk, to listen, to monitor and adjust, and to get help when necessary. You remain unified and connected.

It's important that we think about and identify where we are in our marriages. Be honest. Ask yourself if you are in the *loveseat* with your spouse, or if you are in the *me seat* focusing on your own needs and agenda. In marriage, there are no *his* problem or *her* problem. It is *our problem*. We aren't meant to be in the *me seats* and feeling alone in our marriages. A husband and wife should be unified in the *loveseat*—loving, respecting, and serving one another.

Jesus is the greatest example of how we are supposed to love, respect, and serve each other. Jesus is the embodiment of love and showed us that love is much more about action and commitment than it is about feelings. This is important as it relates to the *loveseat*. We must commit to unity with one another no matter how we are feeling. Jesus pursued us passionately and then displayed the ultimate love by dying in our place on the cross. And the Bible specifically calls husbands to love their wives with that same type of selfless love. Ephesians 5:25 reads, "For husbands, this means love your wives, just as Christ loved the church. He gave up his life for her." (NLT)

Jesus was a king, but He laid down His rights to be served. Instead, he served others. As husbands, we are called to serve our wives. In practical terms, this means placing her needs ahead of our wants and needs. It means prioritizing her ahead of our hobbies or even our careers.

It means being willing to do dishes, fold laundry, or whatever else is needed to support her.

> *"But among you it will be different. Whoever wants to be a leader among you must be your servant, and whoever wants to be first among you must become your slave. For even the Son of Man came not to be served but to serve others and to give his life as a ransom for many."* (Matthew 20:26–28, NLT)

Jesus was described as a shepherd. In His culture, a shepherd was one who would protect the sheep from any form of attack, even if it meant risking his own life in the process. This type of love in action doesn't happen from the me seat. It only happens in the loveseat. As husbands, we are called to be the protectors of our wives, and we can't effectively do this unless we are "all in" and fully committed to the marriage, unified together in the loveseat.

God's Definition of Love

What is love? As men, we often have the misconception that love is a mushy, sappy expression of emotions. We might even secretly believe that being loving is a feminine quality and that men aren't cut out for it. The truth is that love is one of the most heroic and masculine actions you can do. It's something your wife and family needs from you, and it's something you, as a man, need to give and receive—from God and from others.

This chapter (and really, all of marriage) is about love, but there are many different definitions of "love" in our world. Love is the foundation of a marriage, but to apply it properly, we need to begin with an understanding of what love really is. With so many definitions floating around, we'd like to bring it back to the source. God created love, so He is the only One qualified to define it.

The Bible has a lot to say about the subject of love. In fact, love is the main point! Many scriptures help give us a biblical context of love and its meaning, but let's focus on "The Love Chapter" from 1 Corinthians 13. In this timeless passage, the Apostle Paul beautifully and poetically captures the essence of real love. This passage is widely considered to contain the most famous words about love ever written:

> *"Love is patient, love is kind. It does not envy, it does not boast, it is not proud. It does not dishonor others, it is not self-seeking, it is not easily angered, it keeps no record of wrongs. Love does not delight in evil but rejoices with the truth. It always protects, always trusts, always hopes, always perseveres. Love never fails."*
> (1 Corinthians 13:4-8)

These famous words from Scripture aren't just a poetic description of love; they also represent a very practical roadmap to guide your marriage in the right direction. Make a conscious decision to love each other using God's definition of love as described in the verses above. Allow your marriage to be led by love, and you'll always be headed in the right direction!

Let's briefly unpack these verses about love and their practical application in your marriage:

Love is patient and kind, so be patient and kind with each other. Love is not boastful or proud, so refuse to allow the poison of pride to taint your marriage. Love is not self-seeking, so choose to put your spouse's needs ahead of your own. Love is not easily angered, so allow no place for spite or hostility in your relationship. Love keeps no record of wrongs, so allow grace and forgiveness to flow freely. Love rejoices with the truth, so refuse to deceive or keep secrets from each other. Love always protects and perseveres, so never give up on each other!

Love is Not Enough

Love is not enough to make a marriage work. That may sound a little unromantic for a book about love and marriage, but love will never be enough to make a marriage work. Here's why:

The world defines love as a feeling and something we fall in and out of, which means we can lose the love that someone has already given us. This is especially disheartening when it comes to marriage. If love is just a fickle feeling, then how in the world can any of us stay married for life? The truth is, we can't—not if that's all there is to love.

Love (the way the Bible describes it) is rooted in unending commitment, healing, self-sacrifice, and grace. That's real love. That's the kind of love that we want for our marriage—not some wishy-washy, tepid love. We want the kind of love that lasts forever. We bet that's the kind of love you want for your marriage, too.

Real love is always rooted in rock-solid commitment. When we are committed to someone or something, we offer that person or thing plenty of time, attention, and devotion. Sadly, many of us are more committed to our hobbies and jobs than we are to our own families.

When we marry, we commit to love our spouse for all the days of our lives. When we have kids, we are committed to raising our kids to the best of our ability and to never give up on them, no matter what. In friendships, we are committed to being there for our friends in times of need and protecting their reputations. As Christians, we show our love and commitment to Christ by praying, reading the Word, and doing what He's called us to do the very best we can. Love. Is. Commitment.

Living Out the Second Promise: "I Will Love and Cherish You."

Love does for a marriage what breathing does for lungs, so do everything in your power to keep the love alive! Make **time** together a priority. Invest in your **friendship** with one another. Seek new ways to **serve** each other's needs. Through your **words** and your **actions**, consistently communicate your **love**, **adoration**, and **commitment** to one another!

PRAYER FOR TODAY

Jesus, thank you for Your love. I know that Your love makes all love possible. Help me to love You wholeheartedly, so that I'm fully able to love my wife wholeheartedly. I know that she needs to feel adored and loved unconditionally by me. Give me the wisdom to know how to show my love to her the way she needs to see it. Help us grow in our love for You, and for each other, more and more through each season of life. You laid down Your life for Your bride, the Church. Help me love my bride with the same kind of selfless sacrifice.

In Jesus' name,
Amen

FOR JOURNALING AND REFLECTION

- What did I learn about my spouse today?
- What did I learn about myself today?
- What did I learn about the promise, "I will love and cherish you"?
- As a result of what I've learned, I will…

DAY 2 ACTIVITY: ESCAPE THE ORDINARY

*Before we get to today's activity, we're going to give you a **sneak preview of the Day 7** activity because you might need several days to be working on it. Today's reading is all about loving and cherishing your wife. The final activity is going to include reading a "love letter" to your wife in which you share some of the attributes you love about her. Write down words that, perhaps, you've never said out loud to her. The last two journaling questions throughout this book can help you get started. You might be amazed by how much this letter will mean to her! If she's participating in the challenge with you, she'll write a love letter for you as well. These letters might become treasures for you both, so dedicate plenty of time to planning and writing it.

For today's activity, we want you and your wife to plan a getaway together. Pick a date on the calendar and commit to it. Maybe you get away alone together on a regular basis. Maybe you haven't done it in years. Either way, within the next three months, plan a getaway for at least one night somewhere. Together, choose where you'd like to go. The planning and dreaming can be almost as much fun as going! Every couple needs some time away together, so make this happen.

_____

_____

_____

_____

_____

_____

_____

_____

_____

_____

_____

_____

_____

_____

_____

_____

_____

_____

_____

_____

_____

_____

_____

_____

_____

_____

_____

_____

_____

_____

_____

_____

_____

_____

_____

_____

_____

_____

_____

_____

_____

_____

Day 3

FOR BETTER OR FOR WORSE

———

On *The Naked Marriage Podcast*, we recently interviewed our friends Tyler and Alyssa Gordon. They courageously shared a chilling story of childhood trauma. It's a story of unspeakable suffering followed by miraculous healing.

Alyssa and her sister, Kayla, had grown up at our church. They were there almost every Sunday, along with their mom and stepdad. On the surface, they looked like a picture-perfect family. Behind closed doors, however, Alyssa and Kayla were living in a secret hell.

Alyssa shared that from the time she was eight years old until he moved out when she was seventeen, her stepfather had been brutally abusing her sexually. He ruled over her with terror, threatening to kill her if she ever told anyone about his repugnant crimes against her. As Alyssa progressed through her early teenage years, not only did the rape continue, but he even began pimping her out to his friends.

She was forced to do whatever these evil men told her to do. If she ever resisted in any way, she was beaten and terrorized. Her stepfather was an evil man. He played the part of a loving father in public, but behind closed doors, he was inflicting despicable acts of physical, emotional, and sexual abuse.

As Alyssa shared her harrowing story, she talked honestly about how heartbreaking it was in those years of abuse to feel her prayers were being unanswered. God was the only one who saw the pain she was enduring. She cried out to Him daily in her prayers. But during eight years of suffering, those prayers felt unanswered. As her mind, her body, and her innocence were being ravaged by evil men, her faith was being tested as well.

She continued to pray, but she would also ask herself the obvious question, "How could an all-powerful and loving God see what I'm going through and do nothing to intervene?"

Questions and experiences like hers that have caused many people to lose faith over the years. The truth is, there aren't any Christian clichés or platitudes that can neatly explain away the devastating pain of people like Alyssa. Trying to minimize a person's deepest pain by simply telling them to have more faith or by quoting a Bible verse to them seems, ironically, like the least Christ-like approach imaginable.

On this side of heaven, we may never have perfect answers to these messy questions. It's hard to understand where the line intersects between God's sovereign protection and the natural consequences of man's sinful free will. Though theologians have debated these issues for centuries, we're not sure they've ever discovered a theological truth more profound than the simple promise that God is with us in our pain.

Alyssa chose to hold onto that simple promise even on the days when her faith felt fragile. She chose to trust that God is still good, even though she was experiencing the worst of human depravity. Eventually, her nightmare ended. Loved ones—including Tyler, whom she eventually married—helped give her the strength to bring these secrets out into the light. Today her former stepfather is behind bars where he belongs. Alyssa and her family are safe. She'll never again have to fear him.

While many others in similar situations have grown bitter, hardhearted, and faithless as a response to their pain, Alyssa has grown more compassionate, more faithful, and more joyful. While many others choose to stuff their pain down deep where they never speak of it, Alyssa and her sister Kayla found the strength to share their testimonies as a way to give help and hope to other survivors of abuse. These strong women and their families are heroes of ours, and we're truly honored to call them friends.

Some people argue that modern-day miracles don't happen anymore.

We look at people like Alyssa and see her joy, her healing, her happy marriage, and her faith as nothing short of miraculous. It takes a super-natural God and a faith-filled human heart to create the kind of story Alyssa is now living. Her life is a vivid reminder that God's healing power is bigger than our biggest heartbreak. It's a beautiful glimpse of heaven, *where He will wipe every tear from our eyes and make all things new as we experience eternal healing in His presence.* (Revelation 21:1)

We pray you never have to endure the horrors of Alyssa's childhood. But in whatever you face, know that Jesus is with you. Just like the Lord was present in the fiery furnace, the lion's den, the imprisonments of the apostles, and the countless other pains and injustices suffered by the forerunners of our faith in the Bible, God is with you in your pain.

Jesus is present with you in your pain, and He loves you. He will carry you through this. He will make it right someday. He is preparing a place for you in heaven, where there will be no more pain or injustice. If you'll cling to these truths in your darkest hours, you won't need the strength to survive the pain. The Lord's strength will carry you through.

Nearly every marriage faces a dynamic in which one or both spouses have faced past trauma. Perhaps the trauma isn't as severe as what Alyssa endured, but regardless of the specifics, all past pain can cause current pain if we don't face it in a healthy way. Part of what makes Alyssa and Tyler's story so inspiring is that they chose to face this trauma *together.* Tyler gave Alyssa strength, compassion, and support. Alyssa trusted Tyler by confiding in him and allowing him to be a partner in every aspect of her healing journey.

Tyler and Alyssa have overcome remarkable obstacles to forge a rock-solid, happy, and healthy family. They're living proof that it's possi-ble to move forward together— through anything—if you're willing to get the help you need, trust in God's goodness and face every issue in partnership with your spouse.

If you're trying to work through any struggle without your spouse or without God, it's time to stop doing it alone. Don't shut your spouse out. A healthy married couple shares everything—both the good things and the hard things—with each other. With God and each other, your marriage can endure any storm and find healing from any wound.

When Life is Hard

Any kind of hardship can take a toll on our marriage. Financial strain, stress at work, frequent work travel, difficulty with kids, a major illness, broken trust, moving, or problems with extended family are a few common issues that cause a husband and wife to argue, pull away from one another, or otherwise hide things from one another. However, the hard times are when we need each other the most. These are the moments when a "naked marriage" truly shines.

Ashley
In our 20 years of marriage, there have been times when we've experienced various forms of hardship. In the grand scheme of things, our struggles weren't "major," but we both felt the strain, nonetheless. One tough season that comes to mind happened about ten years ago when we decided to move to a new state and a new ministry opportunity. Though willingly leaving a place that we loved, we were very excited about starting our new adventure in a new place.

Even so, the moment we got there, I felt loneliness creeping in. We were staying in a tiny rental right beside some water. It was especially hard since we had two extremely loud and active small boys who couldn't swim yet at the time.

Dave was busy at his new job, and I was trying to hold down the fort at home with two small children. As the months slowly crept by, Dave and I both felt weary and uncomfortable with our new city. It was a tough adjustment. There were even times I felt a bit resentful toward Dave because it seemed like he was adjusting so much better than I was. But I continued to trudge on through the long days at home with my restless boys while feeling a bit lost and alone.

Gradually, the tension between us began to rise. We stopped being intentional about telling each other our true feelings about the move. I think both of us were so exhausted at the end of the day that we just couldn't even find the words. Eventually, this bad habit caught up with us. We both became so edgy towards one another, and we weren't prioritizing date nights or time together like we once did.

The relational dynamic between us was becoming more sinister by the day, and I hated it. I wanted things to be better. I wanted to love where we were living, but I was so homesick and frustrated with the state of things.

One day, I remember Dave coming to me with tired eyes. He grabbed my hands, and he said, "Sweetie, this has been a really hard move for both of us. I don't know why, but it just *is*. What do you think would make things better for us?" I was so relieved to hear him say those words. I wasn't alone in my frustration. Dave felt it too.

Tears welled up in my eyes as I poured out my heart to him. It was as if I was unveiling layers of my mind and heart to him piece by piece, and it felt so good to be emotionally "naked." I told him how much I missed my friends and family. I expressed my frustration with the boys not listening. I asked Dave how things were going at work, and he talked about some frustrations he was experiencing there. I began to really see and understand him on a deeper level because of his willingness to be emotionally "naked" with me.

Neither of us held anything back. It felt so good to just let it all out and to call this season what it really was: *hard*. It was good to know that we both had each other's backs. Friends, when we are going through a tough season, we must resist the urge to face it alone. Don't give resentment an opportunity to take hold of your heart! Instead, commit to sharing with your spouse the whole truth—the good, the bad, and the ugly. All. Of. It. Your openness and honesty will help you both to endure this hard season and keep your marriage strong.

Dave

Husbands, go to your wife and tell her everything you're feeling, and then ask her to do the same. Listen to each other. When you both do this, you will feel the weight being lifted off your shoulders. The two of you are on the *same* team. You win together or lose together. You lean on one another through thick and thin. That's what our marriage commitment is all about. Hard seasons may linger, but you can make it through when you face these times together—hand-in-hand, heart-to-heart, day-by-day, and step-by-step.

How to Overcome a "For Worse" Season

If your marriage is going through a "for worse" season right now, here are a few truths to remember during challenging seasons of life. These have helped us, and we pray they help you as well:

1. **Remember that your *character* should always be stronger than your *circumstances*.**
    We can't always control what happens to us, but we can always control how we choose to respond. In those moments, when we choose to stop complaining and instead give thanks to God for the good in our lives, the negative parts start to seem much less significant. Choose to keep a positive attitude and a thankful heart regardless of what you're going through.

"Rejoice always, pray continually, give thanks in all circumstances; for this is God's will for you in Christ Jesus." (1 Thessalonians 5:16-18)

2. Remember that your struggles always lead to strength.
Every difficulty in your life, whether big or small, is something God will use to produce in you more strength, faith, and perseverance—if you let Him! All your pain has a purpose.

"And we know that in all things God works for the good of those who love him, who have been called according to his purpose." (Romans 8:28)

3. Remember that God's timing is always perfect.
God's plans are almost always different from our plans, but His plans are always perfect! Have the patience to wait on His timing instead of forcing your own.

"For I know the plans I have for you declares the Lord; plans to prosper you and not to harm you, plans to give you hope and a future." (Jeremiah 29:11)

4. Remember that God will never leave your side.
You may feel like you're going through this struggle all alone, but from the moment you ask Jesus to bring you into God's family, He will be by your side to the end. Never lose hope!

"Be strong and courageous. Do not be afraid or terrified because of them, for the Lord your God goes with you; he will never leave you nor forsake you." (Deuteronomy 31:6)

When Life is Good

We expect marriage to be hard when times are hard. However, when we say "for better or for worse," most of us are thinking there won't really be any struggles in the good times. Ironically, success has probably ended as many marriages as tragedy has. That may sound crazy, so let us explain.

We read a news story recently about a married couple in Kentucky who won the lottery. They described it as the "happiest day of their lives." They played the lottery every day and always dreamed about what they'd do if they won. Finally, their numbers came up. In a single moment, they had gone from being flat broke to being millionaires!

Everything changed. At first, it was amazing. They were riding the wave of adrenaline and buying everything they wanted. But it wasn't long before the rush wore off and everything started to crumble. They began to fight about what to do with the money, which led them to become secretive and distrusting of each other. They developed some unhealthy habits because their new wealth gave them the false feeling of invincibility. Ultimately, this "happiest day of their lives" turned to tragedy.

Several short years after winning, the wife had died of a drug overdose, and the husband had become a paranoid recluse in his home. The one statement the newspaper was able to get from him was this sobering warning: "It ruined everything. I wouldn't wish this money on anyone."

The money wasn't the problem. The money just amplified the problems they already had and created some new ones. That might not keep you from trying to get rich quick, but hopefully it gives you a valuable perspective on life—whether you end up rich or broke. People are always more important than possessions, and your commitment to your spouse must always be stronger than your circumstances.

When a couple hasn't built their relationship on faith and commitment, then it is just built on feelings or convenience. Great success can actually expose the weak spots of a marriage because it ultimately reveals our secret motives and the level of our faith. We must never allow any set of circumstances to become more powerful in our life than our unwavering commitment to our spouse.

Whether you're currently in a "better" or "worse" set of circumstances, choose to trust God and support one another. Don't let worry rob you of your peace. Find strength in each other and in the truth of God's promises.

> *"Don't worry about anything; instead, pray about everything. Tell God what you need, and thank him for all he has done. Then you will experience God's peace, which exceeds anything we can understand. His peace will guard your hearts and minds as you live in Christ Jesus."* (Philippians 4:6-7, NLT)

Living out the Third Promise: "I Love You, for Better or for Worse."

If hard times come, we pray that you respond with faith in God and unity in your marriage. When you exchanged your vows and said, "for better or for worse," what you were really saying is, "I'm going to be by your side *no matter what.*"

No matter what life throws your way, you need to be able to say to your spouse: "In good times, I'm going to celebrate with you. In tragic times, I'm going to cry with you. In uncertain times, I'm going to hold you. I'm going to be by your side now and always...no matter what!"

PRAYER FOR TODAY

Lord, help me love, support, and serve my wife in good times and in bad. I know marriage, like all of life, has many good times as well as difficult struggles. In the moments of celebration, help me be my wife's biggest cheerleader. In moments of struggle, help me be a good listener and the safest place on earth for her to process her feelings. Help me fight my instincts to want to "fix" the situation, without taking the time to listen as she processes what she's feeling. Help us praise You in good times and hard times. Help us trust You in good times and hard times. Let us face every victory and every loss hand in hand and side by side.

In Jesus' name,
Amen

FOR JOURNALING AND REFLECTION

- What did I learn about my spouse today?
- What did I learn about myself today?
- What did I learn about the promise, "I love you, for better or for worse"?
- As a result of what I've learned, I will…

DAY 3 ACTIVITY: EMBRACE THE STRUGGLE

Start a conversation with your wife in which you discuss some of the biggest struggles you've faced in your past and in your present. Then, discuss how you would both hope to respond to specific struggles in your future. First, ask and answer these questions:

1. What was the biggest struggle you faced before we got married? How did you overcome it?
2. What do you believe is the biggest struggle we have overcome in our marriage?
3. What is the biggest struggle we are facing in our marriage right now?

Looking ahead to the future...

1. How do you hope we would respond if we went bankrupt?
2. How do you hope we would respond if one of us was diagnosed with a serious illness?

Finally, ask each other these questions:

1. How can I help you through the struggles you're facing?
2. How can we be better partners in facing our struggles as a team?

_____

_____

_____

_____

_____

_____

_____

_____

_____

_____

_____

_____

_____

_____

_____

_____

_____

_____

_____

_____

_____

_____

_____
_____
_____
_____
_____
_____
_____
_____
_____
_____
_____
_____
_____
_____
_____
_____
_____
_____
_____

Day 4

FOR RICHER OR FOR POORER

———

PHILIPPIANS 4:12-13

S tress related to money is one of the biggest causes of divorce. When the finances are unstable, it can make the entire marriage feel unstable. One reason couples often fight about money is the fact that one partner is a "spender" while the other is a "saver." Obviously, this can cause arguments. In some marriages, *both* spouses are spenders, and the relationship is under constant financial strain. No matter the scenario, any couple can find themselves under financial pressure from time to time.

My parents struggled financially in the early years of my life, but they still managed to give me some very memorable gifts. They bought me my first bicycle, my first Nintendo, and even a New Kids on the Block cassette tape (which is what we had in the "old days" before CD players and iPods.) Most of those gifts ended up in a dumpster, but several gifts have endured through the years and made a permanent impact on my life and faith. Among those "enduring gifts" was the blessing of growing up with two parents who truly loved and supported each other.

Financially, my parents are very successful today, but my family was very poor around the time when I was five years old. One of my brothers was three, and my youngest brother was a baby. The economy was terrible, and like many young parents, my mom and dad struggled to make ends meet.

One day, Dad came home and found Mom crying while holding my crying baby brother. Though a very tenderhearted woman, she almost never cried, so Dad knew something was terribly wrong. He asked her what was going on. Through her tears, she pointed to the refrigerator and said, "There's no milk, and there's no money to buy more."

My parents, who are two of the hardest-working and most resourceful people on the planet, found themselves looking into the eyes of their hungry children. They felt the desperation of not knowing how to provide their most basic needs. Dad looked through the house for any spare change, but there was none to be found. There was no credit card. There was no cash. There was simply nothing.

Dad had a thought and rushed into his bedroom. He opened his sock drawer and pulled out two shiny silver dollars. They had been given to him by his great grandmother when he was a young boy. They were all he had left of her memory, but despite their great sentimental value—and potential financial value—their only value at that moment was that they might meet a need for his family.

Without hesitation, Dad walked to the store, grabbed a gallon of milk, and slapped those two silver dollars on the counter. That's what love looks like. Loving your spouse "for richer or for poorer" means being willing to make selfless sacrifices to provide for your family.

I told this story in a sermon at church recently, and my parents happened to be sitting in the crowd. I got to the end and found myself gripped by emotion as I reflected on a lifetime of love and support I've received from them both. I looked down and saw that they were crying too. I told them I loved them.

Mom and Dad have loved and supported each other through every season of their marriage. Since those early struggles, they've had great financial prosperity, but their values have remained completely unwavering whether they've been in a "richer" or a "poorer" scenario. Their example has taught me to have a healthy view of money. Even more importantly, their love for each other is what gave me a healthy view of marriage. I'm truly thankful for their continuing legacy of faith, family, and love.

God Wants You to Have a Healthy View of Money

Whether or not your parents set a positive example for you, it's so important that you learn a healthy view of finances. So much marital stress can be traced back to financial stress. Whether you're rich or poor, developing a unified financial plan with your spouse can bring freedom and peace to your marriage. My friends Mike and Allie are living proof!

Mike and Allie were living "The American Dream," which basically means they were living beyond their means. This young family was buried in debt and trying to keep their heads above water on a school-teacher's salary. The debt was creating stress that was putting a heavy strain on their marriage and young family.

They decided that something had to change, so they took action. They researched the Bible's timeless wisdom on finances and adjusted their spending, saving, and giving accordingly. A few years later, they had experienced a dramatic turnaround and are now debt-free! They're living in a freedom that they never had before. Now they coach others to help them discover the same financial freedom and peace.

Jesus taught more about money than he talked about Heaven and Hell. He knew that a healthy view of money would be vital to developing a healthy view of life and marriage. If I could sum up the Bible's many teachings on money into one statement, I'd say it's this: *"Money is a good servant, but a poor master."*

Early in our marriage, Ashley and I made some "rookie mistakes" when it came to money. We took on unnecessary debt, overspent, and didn't save. Those decisions created a lot of stress that wise choices could have prevented. We finally learned that a commitment to financial freedom can bring freedom and peace to all other aspects of life and marriage. Here are the principles I wish we had practiced from the very beginning.

1. **Relentlessly eliminate your debt.**

   Financial debt has caused more fights between husbands and wives than nearly any other subject. It can have a suffocating impact because it removes options and replaces freedoms with constraints. Do whatever you can do to remove debt. Then avoid taking on new debt. Remember that a "new car smell" is nice, but it's nothing compared to the debt-free scent of a paid-for car!

   "The rich rule over the poor, and the borrower is slave to the lender." (Proverbs 22:7)

2. **Wisely plan your spending.**

   For a lot of people, the word "budget" is a bad word that makes their skin crawl just to speak it. To be completely transparent with you, we've always been bad at budgeting. But over the years, we've come to see the benefit of developing a spending plan. A budget is simply a way of telling your money where to go instead of watching your money fly out the window. It puts you back in control, which brings peace and helps you discover that you don't actually need a lot of the stuff you've been buying.

   Then Jesus said to them, "Watch out! Be on your guard against all kinds of greed; life does not consist in an abundance of posses-sions." (Luke 12:15)

3. **Systematically prioritize your saving.**

   There is more peace in my marriage when we have a little finan-cial cushion in the bank. It gives reassurance to my wife that, if an unexpected expense comes our way, we won't have to go sell one of our kidneys on the black market to cover it. When you save a little money out of every check, you'll be building a nest egg that removes unnecessary stress from your marriage.

"Dishonest money dwindles away, but whoever gathers money little by little makes it grow." (Proverbs 13:11)

4. **Joyfully increase your giving.**

For all our many financial mistakes in those early years of marriage, we did do one thing right when it came to our finances. We chose to follow the Bible's clear teaching to tithe—giving the first 10 percent of our income to fund Christian ministry—and to be generous to those in need. That choice has brought more blessings to us than I can describe, and I hope you will also experience the joy generosity brings.

The happiest couples I know are extremely generous. The most miserable couples I know are misers. Don't be a Scrooge! When you're wise with your money, it will put you in the position to be generous with your money and generosity always brings joy.

"Each of you should give what you have decided in your heart to give, not reluctantly or under compulsion, for God loves a cheerful giver." (2 Corinthians 9:7)

5. **Eternally maximize your investments.**

It's important to have a retirement plan, but it's even more important to invest into causes that will create an eternal legacy. Don't just think of your money in terms of what you'll do with it from paycheck to paycheck; plan out what you'll do with your money that will impact generations to come. When your money is in the right place, your heart will be in the right place.

"Do not store up for yourselves treasures on earth, where moths and

vermin destroy, and where thieves break in and steal. But store up
for yourselves treasures in heaven, where moths and vermin do not
destroy, and where thieves do not break in and steal. For where
your treasure is, there your heart will be also." (Matthew 6:19-21)

The Myth of "More"

When our oldest son, Cooper, was born, somebody gave us a DVD of
baby sign language that we started showing him when he was just a
few months old. As new parents, we had no idea what we were doing,
but we thought that if our baby learned sign language, then everybody
would assume we really knew our stuff!

The DVD didn't make him a fluent phenomenon in signing, but
it did teach him something. It turned out there was one sign that he
picked up and consistently used. He knew what it meant, and he used
it often: the sign for the word "more." Before he could speak a word, he
had already discovered the instinctive human fascination with *more*.

Babies just want more milk, or more toys, but as humans grow,
the hunger for more grows. In adulthood, most of us are fueled by the
drive for more money, more success, more pleasure, more fun, more
rest, more sex and more of pretty much everything else. Our materi-
alistic, hedonistic culture convinces us that we're not happy, but if we
just buy a little more of a certain product, then we will be. It's a vicious
cycle that never ends until we discover a life-changing principle from
the truth of God's Word.

Here's the truth: "More" will never make you happy. It's a myth. It's
an empty pursuit. **Contentment isn't a result of having more; it's a
result of wanting less**. Until you're content with what you've already
got, you will never be content—no matter how much you get!

God wants you to live in a spirit of gratitude and contentment. Don't let the selfishness of this world rob you of that. Choose to give thanks in all circumstances and be truly content with what you already have, and the "more" that comes your way will just be the icing on the cake. God has many more blessings in store for you, but you won't be able to fully embrace them until you're willing to trade more of this world for more of God.

If you are willing to apply these principles to your faith, and your finances, your marriage will be stronger no matter how much money you happen to have in the bank.

The Secret to Real Contentment

It's so easy to fall into the trap of thinking more money would instantly fix all of our problems, but King Solomon proves this isn't the case! Solomon was one of the wealthiest, wisest, and most successful people to ever live. He literally had anything and everything he desired, except for one thing: happiness. In the Bible, the book of Ecclesiastes records Solomon's frustrations:

> "I denied myself nothing my eyes desired; I refused my heart no pleasure. My heart took delight in all my labor, and this was the reward for all my toil. Yet when I surveyed all that my hands had done and what I had toiled to achieve, everything was meaningless, a chasing after the wind; nothing was gained under the sun."
> (Ecclesiastes 2:10-11)

Solomon's problem started when he strayed away from God's design for marriage as being a lifelong, committed, monogamous partnership to one person. He allowed his culture to redefine his views. He ended up with hundreds of wives and hundreds more concubines. He thought sex, success, and stuff would make him happy, but it never does.

The deepest longings of your heart can only be fulfilled when you make the countercultural choice to trust God's plan for your life and your marriage. His plans for you and your marriage are perfect, and whether you're facing good times or bad, for better or for worse, you and your spouse can discover true contentment. You can come to understand the words of the Apostle Paul who said,

> *"I know how to live on almost nothing or with everything. I have learned the secret of living in every situation, whether it is with a full stomach or empty, with plenty or little. For I can do everything through Christ, who gives me strength."* (Philippians 4:12-13, NLT)

Living Out the Fourth Promise: "I Will Love You, For Richer or For Poorer."

If you lack peace in your finances right now, make a plan of action to start in a new direction. Get "naked"—or honest—with one another about the state of your finances. Don't live beyond your means. Refuse to allow financial stress (whether pressure from a lack of resources or greed from an abundance of resources) rob you of joy and contentment. Work together to create goals for debt reduction and generosity. Dream about ways to create a legacy for future generations through your finances, your faith, and your love for one another.

PRAYER FOR TODAY

Lord, help me have a wise view of money. As a man, you wired me to be a provider, but I'm also prone to look at money as a source of identity instead of looking to You. Help me provide well for my family, but help me also realize that You are the ultimate Provider. Remind me to encourage and affirm my wife in the work she does as well. Don't let me wear myself out chasing wealth. Give me the discipline to make wise financial decisions, since it all belongs to You, and I'm merely a manager of it temporarily. Help me make my wife and family feel secure in our finances, but let us never worship money or the things it can buy. Whether in great prosperity or great need, help us trust You completely and praise You. Help me remember relationships are of far greater value than money. May I always show my wife that she's more valuable to me than all the money in the world.

In Jesus' name,
Amen

FOR JOURNALING AND REFLECTION

- What did I learn about my spouse today?
- What did I learn about myself today?
- What did I learn about the promise, "I will love you, for richer or for poorer"?
- As a result of what I've learned, I will…

DAY 4 ACTIVITY: SET SOME GOALS

Take an assessment of your current financial situation. Talk about things you're doing well and things you'd like to reprioritize. Each of you choose one financial goal you'd like to achieve in the next year and also one financial goal you'd like to achieve in your lifetimes. Dream about how life could look once those goals are achieved. Talk about specific ways you could start moving towards those goals. Don't blame each other for your current financial strains. Find ways to work together to bring solutions. Create one new shared dream or financial goal for your future. If time permits, we also encourage you to listen to episode 50 on *The Naked Marriage Podcast* entitled "Choosing Your Spouse Over Money."

_____

_____

_____

_____

_____

_____

_____

_____

_____

_____

_____

_____

_____

_____

_____

_____

_____

_____

_____

_____

Day 5

FORSAKING ALL OTHERS

———

RUTH 1:16-17

The strongest marriages are built on a foundation of love, vulnerability, and commitment. The strength of your commitment will always determine the strength of your marriage. God's definition of marriage is rooted in the concept of commitment and faithfulness. When you said, "I do," to your spouse, you weren't just expressing your current feelings; you were making a promise of commitment that will ultimately be your legacy of love.

Marriage, by its very nature, is a conscious choice to selflessly put the needs of your spouse ahead of your own preferences or comforts. No marriage can survive unless it is rooted in rock-solid commitment and honest vulnerability.

As a pastor for many years, I had the privilege of officiating wedding ceremonies. It's such an honor to stand in that sacred moment with a bride and groom as they exchange vows and rings and enter into the holy covenant of marriage. One of the Bible passages I often read at wedding ceremonies comes from Ruth 1:16–17:

> But Ruth replied, "Don't ask me to leave you and turn back. Wherever you go, I will go; wherever you live, I will live. Your people will be my people, and your God will be my God. Wherever you die, I will die, and there I will be buried. May the Lord punish me severely if I allow anything but death to separate us!" (NLT)

These words beautifully capture the commitment necessary for a strong marriage. God wants to create a generational impact through your marriage. The level at which your marriage will make an eternal impact is defined by your level of commitment to the *naked marriage*. There is no relationship more sacred than your marriage, so treasure your spouse. Never let anyone or anything take the place of priority your spouse should hold in your heart. Make sure your marriage is built on a foundation of rock-solid commitment to God and to each other.

A marriage thrives when a couple remembers to put each other first. A marriage can crumble when one or both spouses strays from their covenant commitment to each other. In our work, we've seen so many couples deal with the aftermath of infidelity and the immeasurable pain it can cause in a marriage.

Life was good for Jason and Jennifer. They'd just had their first child a few months earlier. They had that look of both excitement and exhaustion that all new parents seem to have. Life seemed to be rolling along just fine for them—until the day a bombshell dropped. Nobody saw it coming.

Jason gave me a call late one night and told me that he had to talk to me. I could sense the urgency in his voice, which was out of character because he was one of the most laid-back guys I knew. My own heart was racing as I drove to meet with him. I had no idea what to expect and was shocked by the news he gave me.

With tears in his eyes, he started to tell me a story that I knew was not going to have a happy ending. He talked about this young woman at work who had been a good "friend" to him. They would work long hours with each other and really felt a close connection. She was married, too, but didn't seem happy in her marriage. At this point, I knew where the story was heading, but I let him finish telling it.

Their "friendship" escalated, and their conversations began to deepen to personal issues. Those close conversations led to hugs which led to… well, you probably know the rest. He cheated on his wife.

Jason was desperate for a way to fix this mess. His wife already knew, and her joy and dreams about their family's future came crashing down in a single moment. His life seemed like it was over.

As I listened to him talk, I honestly didn't know whether I should give him a hug to encourage him or punch him in the face for being an idiot. I decided to hug him. I had seen this familiar scene play in the lives of others, and I knew his consequences were going to be painful enough without me adding to them.

In the months that followed, Jason made drastic steps to rebuild his broken marriage and regain his wife's trust. I met with him regularly for accountability and support. He cut off all conversation with the other woman and even sought a job transfer so he wouldn't be near her. He knew that putting distance between him and this other woman was the only way for his marriage to have a chance of survival.

The survival of their marriage is a miracle that can only be explained by the Grace of God. But even in that victory, the sad reality is that their marriage will never be the same. Even with great days ahead, there will always be deep scars and damaged trust.

Infidelity Can Take Many Forms

"Infidelity" is a word we typically use to refer to a sexual affair, but the word itself simply means "to break trust." There are many ways to break trust and be unfaithful in marriage beyond a sexual affair. To truly be faithful and committed in marriage, we must remain accountable for any temptations or addictions that could undermine the intimacy and unity in our marriage.

Ashley

One night, I received a desperate call from a dear friend of mine. When I answered, she was sobbing and gasping for air to form words. My heart sank. I felt a lump in my throat. I asked her what was going on, and if she was okay. When she finally caught her breath, she told me her husband, who had been clean and sober for years, had a relapse. Understandably, my friend was devastated, angry, confused, and heartbroken. They had been through so much in their five years of marriage, and she had finally felt like he was settled and stable. They had even waited to have children until he had been clean and sober for a significant amount of time. Now, they had a toddler and a baby on the way. After a long pause and a lot of tears, my friend said,

"How could he do this to us? I'm not sure if I can walk through the process of sobriety again or if I can ever trust him again. What am I supposed to do now?"

Dave

Have you ever found yourself at a crossroads like this one? Maybe addiction isn't the struggle. Maybe your wife has a problem with deceit or not telling the whole truth. Maybe she struggles with depression or anxiety. Or, maybe your spouse has a debilitating illness that goes in and out of remission. Whether the struggle is something she actively brought on herself or is no fault of her own, it can feel like you are drowning under the weight of the burden. It can even feel like you are just waiting for the other shoe to drop, and for everything to fall apart any day. You're shell-shocked by the trauma that you walked through with your spouse, and you don't know if you have it in you to support her through the struggle again.

If you've ever felt this way, I want you to know that you are not alone. It's human to feel helpless at times. Sometimes we don't know what to say or do to make things better. The truth is, sometimes things get worse before they get better. It's messy and unpredictable, but we still have hope. We serve a God who makes masterpieces out of the messiest, most dire situations. Please know that I am not stating this as some pie-in-the-sky blanket response. I know this to be true because I have lived it.

Ashley

Early in our marriage, I found out that Dave had been hiding a pornography addiction from me. When I accidentally found these awful sites on our family computer in our basement, I couldn't believe what I saw. My mind couldn't even fathom who had looked at these. At first, I was completely in denial that my husband had been the culprit. However, I felt the Holy Spirit gently opening my eyes and heart to this hard truth. I knew that I had to address this with Dave right away. I called him at work, and when he answered, all I could say was, "Hey, Sweetie. Do you have something that you need to tell me?"

There was a long pause, but then, with a tremble in his voice, he confessed to everything. He apologized repeatedly. He said it was like his best day and worst day all rolled into one. He had been living in shame and bondage to this porn addiction for years. Now, we had to weather the storm of beating this addiction. At that time, I didn't realize how hard the journey would be and how much it would push me to my breaking point.

In the days that followed, we moved our computer out of our basement and into a public space in our home. We put accountability and website filtering software on our computer and devices. We also had a lot of open, honest, and often awkward conversations to make sure we weren't keeping any secrets, so the temptation and shame of porn wouldn't get a foothold on Dave once again.

Things began to improve. I started to trust Dave once again. We regained our intimacy with one another, and I could see our marriage growing stronger from this hardship. However, about six months into Dave's healing process, he confessed that he had relapsed and looked at porn a few times. I was heartbroken. In fact, I was a little angry at God. I prayed angry prayers like this: *"God, we are doing everything You'd have us do, so why is Dave still struggling with this? Is he ever really going to be rid of it? Is it me? Am I not enough for him? Is our relationship damaged beyond repair?"*

Dave was remorseful and disgusted by his behavior. I knew we were at a critical tipping point in our marriage. As a young woman who hadn't been married very long, I honestly didn't know what to say or do. However, I knew I needed to pray. Through my anger, heartbrokenness, and frustration, I asked God to help me forgive Dave. I knew this forgiveness was necessary first before I gave him the chance to regain my trust. I asked God to help me find the courage for me to convey my true feelings about this relapse to Dave, but also to give me compassion to unveil my feelings in the most loving way possible. I asked God to take this addiction from my husband—to get rid of these images that both tempted him and haunted his mind. I asked God to restore the trust and intimacy that the enemy was so clearly trying to take from our marriage. Little by little, day by day, week by week, month by month, I saw God transform my husband and our marriage. At the same time, He also refined my heart.

I realized I could be angry and disappointed with the sin in my husband's life while still offering him my forgiveness. I was confronted with my own sinful nature and frailties that God had so graciously forgiven. As God forgave me, I also needed to forgive my repentant husband. I understood that two are better than one, and if we wanted to have a "naked marriage," we needed to understand that it is never "his struggle" or "her struggle." It is always "our struggle." We weather storms so much better when we choose to endure them together. I learned that God truly can make a masterpiece out of our mess when we bring our chaos to Him and trust Him with it.

God brought so much good out of that hard season. Though I wouldn't want to walk through it again, I am thankful for how God clearly showed His power and mercy in our lives and brought us closer to Him and one another.

So, when my heartbroken friend's husband relapsed, and she asked me, "What am I supposed to do now?" I told her what I had learned through my seasons of marital hardship. I told her she doesn't have to say the "right words" because it's more about the tone she uses and her physical and emotional presence. These supportive gestures will help her husband find the help that he needs to get clean once again. I warned that her feelings are going to be all over the place, but she can't allow them to be her compass. Only God—and those who love Him, love us, and love our spouse—can lead us on the right path to healing.

I also said not to get discouraged because if God has brought her husband to sobriety before, He can do it again. He is never finished with us, and He will use everything—even relapses, broken promises, and disappointments—for our good and His glory. My friend did all those things and stayed by her husband's side. Today, her husband has been clean and sober for two years and even helps others get clean as well. Most importantly, their marriage is stronger than ever.

Dave

If you feel overwhelmed by your wife's struggles, take heart and know that God is with you and your spouse through this. He sees your pain and frustration. He wants to comfort you and give you the courage and strength to get through this hard season together. So, be honest with your wife. Hold tight to one another. Get the help that you and your spouse need, whether it be from a Christian counselor, support group like Celebrate Recovery, or from a doctor for medical needs. Reach out for help. Bottom line: Don't give up. You both will get through this because God will give you a renewed strength to face each day together.

Living Out the Fifth Promise: "I Will Love You Faithfully, Forsaking All Others."

We protect everything that's important to us. We lock our houses and our cars because we don't want them stolen or vandalized. We keep our money in the bank because they have a vault and armed guards. We protect our most valuable things from anyone who would harm them.

You need to see your marriage as a priceless treasure that must be protected at all costs. There are many in the world that would steal it or harm it, and you are responsible for keeping it safe. Do whatever you can to build safeguards around your marriage. Specifically, do everything in your power to protect your marriage from infidelity! Show your wife that you have eyes only for her.

Make every effort to build an affair-proof marriage. Come clean about any secrets you've been keeping from your spouse—including pornography. Build your marriage on a foundation of trust. When trust has been broken, work together to promote forgiveness, healing, and time to rebuild trust.

PRAYER FOR TODAY

Lord, in a world of sexual brokenness and temptation, please help me maintain sexual purity and integrity. Give me the strength to withstand the visual temptations all around me. Please let my eyes and my heart be drawn only to my wife. Help me honor her and be faithful to her physically and emotionally. Help me make her feel safe, adored, and forever beautiful in my eyes. Let my love and commitment give her confidence. Preserve the trust in our relationship and safeguard us from any temptations that would divide us.

In Jesus' name,
Amen

FOR JOURNALING AND REFLECTION

- What did I learn about my spouse today?
- What did I learn about myself today?
- What did I learn about the promise, "I will love you faithfully, forsaking all others"?
- As a result of what I've learned, I will…

DAY 5 ACTIVITY: SPICE THINGS UP

In today's (or tonight's) activity, focus on your sex life. "Forsaking all others" isn't just about avoiding an affair, although that's obviously important. It's also about prioritizing sex within your marriage.

Today, have a conversation together specifically about sex. Talk about what you like. Talk about something new you might enjoy trying together in the bedroom. Be honest about your hang-ups, insecurities, past hurts, temptations, body image issues, and anything else that might impact the sexual intimacy within your marriage. Give your spouse specific compliments. Reaffirm your desire for each other.

Once you've discussed your sex life, you've only completed the first part of the assignment. Part two is to actually make love. Let there be some time between the conversation and the actual lovemaking so that you can both reflect on the words that were spoken earlier. Emotional intimacy began to develop from your conversation. Let it now transition to physical/sexual intimacy. Remember, better communication is a huge key to better sex.

If time permits, we also encourage you to listen to episode 52 of *The Naked Marriage Podcast*, which is entitled "Sexpectations Part 1."

Day 6

IN SICKNESS AND IN HEALTH

ECCLESIASTES 4:9-12

Health challenges can cause physical, emotional, and financial strains in a marriage. Learning to lean on your spouse through health hardships can actually bring great strength and intimacy into your marriage. We've seen this in the many couples we've worked with over the years, but it hit home when I faced an unexpected health challenge.

I have always hated going to doctor's offices. I usually spend a half hour filling out the same forms I filled out at the last visit and then waiting at least a half hour past my scheduled appointment time just to be weighed and prodded like livestock. Then I would be told that I need to either lose twenty pounds or grow six inches taller to be at a healthy weight on their demoralizing body mass index chart. After the subtle fat-shaming, I'd be stuck in another waiting room for the actual doctor to enter. Once I do see the doctor, he/she goes through their regular litany of questions, looks inside my ears (for some reason) before abruptly sending me back to the front desk to cover the overpriced co-pay for the whole experience.

Don't get me wrong: I respect the medical profession. My mom was a hospice nurse, and seeing her work inspired me as a child. As I'm writing these words, our world is still dealing with the COVID-19 pandemic and healthcare workers are on the frontlines of the battle, doing heroic work to keep us safe. I understand why doctors are vital. I've just personally never liked the experience of going to see them. I'm more likely to stay at home and take some Advil when I'm feeling sick. Usually, my approach works out fine, and the issue resolves itself before I ever have to see a professional.

This approach has worked well for most of my life, and I remained relatively healthy, with little medical oversight, through my twenties and the first half of my thirties. But when I hit my mid-thirties, I noticed that my body wasn't working quite like it had before. I chalked up this slight decline to the expected physical effects of aging. My amazing wife wisely realized it was something else entirely.

Ashley is the smart one in our relationship. Over the course of the twenty years we've been together, I've learned to trust her instincts even more than my own. Still, my stubbornness gets in the way sometimes, and when she started suggesting that I go to a doctor to get some testing done, I resisted. I made every excuse imaginable and told her that I'd make a few tweaks to my diet. I told myself everything would work itself out.

Things got worse instead of better. My energy level was shot, my thinking wasn't clear, my digestive system felt like it was going to explode, and I had a myriad of other issues, both big and small. I finally relented and went to the doctor. The normal routine at the doctor's office yielded few results. I was basically prescribed medication to help with digestion.

Over time, the digestion medicine seemed to be doing little to solve the issues. I went to some specialists to have an ultrasound of my stomach and gallbladder. I also had an endoscopy to put a scope down my throat into my stomach. I was certain they were going to find a giant tumor in my gut because of the pressure I felt there, but they found nothing.

The doctors pivoted their diagnosis from digestive-related issues to stress-related issues. I was told that stress was the main factor in all my ailments. This might have been partially true and what ultimately triggered the genetic time-bomb of what turned out to be a thyroid disorder. I was living with a lot of stress trying to balance family time with four energetic kids, plus two different jobs. My pace was unsustainable, and my body seeming to systematically shut down was possibly my body's way (and possibly God's way) of getting my attention.

I went to see a Christian counselor for therapy, which proved to be incredibly helpful. I highly recommend counseling to anyone whether they're dealing with a thyroid issue or not. It's healthy to talk through our struggles with someone trained to help us process them. I'm very thankful for that experience, and all I gained through it, but my physical symptoms saw very little improvement. There was clearly something wrong inside my body that needed to be identified and resolved.

After at least a year of dead ends with doctors and specialists, Ashley made me an appointment at a new doctor's office. Ashley had visited this office previously and had a good experience. She encouraged me to give it a try. I reluctantly submitted to her persistent advice, and I made the appointment.

They ran a wide-spectrum lab test of my bloodwork, looking for anything at all that could be out of balance. I honestly didn't expect anything to come back from the blood tests. Every other appointment had been a waste of time, and I expected this one to be the same. When the results came in, I was simultaneously shocked by the results and somewhat relieved to finally have some answers.

The doctor explained to me that I had Hashimoto's Disease, an auto-immune disease that can cause hypothyroidism. In layman's terms, she explained what that meant and how it could be treated. In addition to my thyroid issues, I had a Vitamin D deficiency and low testosterone. She explained that these other issues might be directly related to the thyroid and that if we could get the thyroid balanced, the rest of my body would probably get more balanced as a result.

I asked what I needed to do to return to full health and get my thyroid working correctly. In addition to a daily dose of medication—which I'd probably have to take for the rest of my life—she outlined an array of lifestyle adjustments that seemed like they would upend every part of my diet and schedule. In the discouragement of the moment, it felt like a death sentence. While she was incredibly cordial, compassionate, and professional, it still felt like she had walked into the room, punched me in the throat, and then kicked me in the crotch. I asked her how long I would deal with this. Her using the word "lifelong" to describe my condition hit me like a knockout blow.

I limped out of the office with a prescription for Synthroid and a library of pamphlets and resources on all the lifestyle changes that would be necessary to combat my thyroid issues. I called Ashley on the way home and calmly tried to explain how we finally had some answers, but we also had a long road ahead. As always, she was incredibly supportive. Hearing her reassuring voice was all I needed in that moment to feel very optimistic about the future.

Like many of our marriage stories, Ashley was a hero in this situation. It was her urging and persistence that ultimately led to my diagnosis. It has been her encouragement that helped me through it. When I was first diagnosed, she responded with such compassion. She prayed with me and patiently listened as I vented and complained. She also helped me laugh. In the early days, she texted me a homemade GIF of Mr. Miyagi from *The Karate Kid* movies saying, "Don't worry, David-san, we will fight Hashimoto together!"

She knows how to get me. I love *The Karate Kid* movies. I love funny gifs. I love to laugh. While we were facing something serious, it was a beautiful way to remind ourselves that we were not going to lose our sense of humor. In fact, our sense of humor would be one of our most important weapons in the fight ahead.

Being able to laugh helps you reclaim power from something that might have taken some power from you. It's brings levity and perspective. It's a workout for your abs without having to do crunches or planks. Plus, it just feels good to laugh. Ashley has helped me through this journey in so many ways, but I wasn't laughing the day I received the results of my blood work.

I started off with an enthusiastic and optimistic game plan, but I went through a little bit of an identity crisis when my diagnosis started sinking in. All this happened when I was thirty-eight years old, and I think it might also have triggered a mild midlife crisis. I went from seeing myself as a strong, virile guy in my prime to seeing myself as an aged, frail, tired old man with a "pre-existing condition."

Only a few years earlier, I had run a marathon and competed in a strenuous "mud run" obstacle course at a nearby Army base. I'd been serious about physical training. Most days, I felt pretty invincible. Now, only a few short years later, I'd lost the will to do much exercising and felt weak and emasculated.

My low testosterone was part of the problem. Not only was "Low T" a real factor in hurting my strength, energy levels, and sex drive, but it also had a psychological effect. Low T can be linked to mental issues such as anxiety and depression, which I was feeling for the first time in my life. I also wrestled with the stigma of seeing my manhood defined by a number, and that number being so low. I would ask myself the vulnerable question, "Am I even a real man anymore?"

Ashley and Jesus worked together to remind me of my true identity and my true manhood. God's promises, combined with an amazingly supportive and encouraging partner in Ashley, made all the difference. In any struggle you face in marriage, if you face it trusting in God and in full partnership with your spouse, there's truly nothing you can't get through. The struggles will make your marriage stronger if you'll face them together, support each other, trust in God's promises, and not lose your sense of humor. I'm so thankful Ashley has reminded me of these truths in both the good times and the difficult days too.

When Health Issues Impact Your Sex Life

I vividly remember the awkward moments of sex education in middle school. Every kid in class was blushing and giggling as our teacher tried to keep a straight face while pointing out the various sex organs and what they do. I remember the charts and the terms. I'll never forget those lessons about words like *penis, vagina, fallopian tubes, ovaries, testicles,* etc. I still blush and giggle a bit even as I type these words out. I suppose we all still have an inner middle-schooler inside, no matter how old we get.

For all those biological terms, there was one body part I'm positive was NOT on any of the teacher's pictures or lists: *thyroid.* I had no idea that the thyroid is a sex organ, but apparently, it is. I've discovered in my own experience that a thyroid disorder can have a negative impact on your sex life. My experience isn't unique. Many people struggling with thyroid disorders and autoimmune diseases of all kinds have reported negative side effects in the bedroom.

Sexual side effects are among the most intimate, frustrating, and embarrassing of any health issues a person can face. It's relatively easy to say, "My thyroid doesn't work." It's something else entirely to say, "My penis doesn't work."

As a guy who coaches thousands of couples worldwide on issues related to marriage and sex—and as a guy who has had a voraciously strong sex drive for most of my life—I never thought I'd personally experience any kind of sexual dysfunction. My thyroid condition, with its accompanying plunge in my testosterone levels, changed all that. In addition to an overall drop in energy and mood, I also experienced a precipitous drop in my sex drive and even impediments in my body's ability to perform. Ashley was incredibly encouraging through this, but I was angry, embarrassed, frustrated, and at times even horrified at times. It's a sense of disappointment and powerlessness I wouldn't wish on anybody.

It's vulnerable and personal to write about this experience, but I know so many others are struggling, so I'm sharing this to give you hope. I've actively been working through the mental, physical, and hormonal issues impacting our sex life, and I've seen great progress. Briefly, sex was something I actually dreaded because of my anxiety of being able to perform. Now, as it's been for most of our marriage, sex is a gift that I always enjoy and look forward to.

What helped me return to a healthy sex life were simple approaches like patience and creating a safe space in our bedroom where there was never any shame or discouragement. I also actively pursued exercise and supplements to help naturally boost my testosterone. I was prescribed hormone therapy by my doctor, but I never actually took it because I was concerned about the side effects. Thankfully, I've been able to bring my testosterone levels back into the normal range through over-the-counter supplements, exercise, and overall health.

I'm pretty much back to normal, but it hasn't just been through supplements and exercise. What has really helped the most has been Ashley's encouragement and support. Her encouragement makes me "feel like the man," even on days when my body feels exhausted and broken. Her words and wisdom are a gift. People underestimate the power of words in your sex life. Her reassurance helped me through some of my most insecure moments, and together, we've forged a path forward in our marriage—both inside and outside the bedroom.

How to Respond When You or Your Wife Becomes Sick

Sickness can run the gamut from a simple cold to a life-threatening illness. In either scenario, we have an opportunity to show great love, kindness, and patience to our spouse. The longer the illness lingers, the harder it becomes. I have seen the hardship of a serious illness nearly destroy the love and respect between a couple, but I have also seen couples come together with tremendous love, faith, and unity to support one another and overcome the sickness.

Some of you might be fighting a major disease right now. My heart and prayers go out to you and your family. No matter what the doctors or test results tell you, I want you to know there is hope. I love these Bible verses that poignantly speak to this issue:

> *"Two are better than one,*
> *because they have a good return for their labor:*
> *If either of them falls down,*
> *one can help the other up.*
> *But pity anyone who falls*
> *and has no one to help them up.*
> *Also, if two lie down together, they will keep warm.*
> *But how can one keep warm alone?*
> *Though one may be overpowered,*
> *two can defend themselves.*
> *A cord of three strands is not quickly broken."*
> (Ecclesiastes 4:9-12)

A husband and wife are going to experience various trials throughout a marriage—many that they never see coming. Regardless of how dire it may seem; we must come together and help one another. God gave us a great gift in one another, and He is with us. This "cord of three strands"— which we addressed early in this study and which is described in the verse above—is you, your spouse, and God. There is tremendous hope when all three are tightly intertwined.

Whether you are going through a season of illness right now or you are both currently healthy, here are seven important things to do when your spouse is sick:

1. Acknowledge the illness

When your spouse is sick, the worst thing you can do is act like this problem doesn't exist. You must acknowledge the pain your wife is in and the fear that anyone has when facing a major illness. Stay close and offer encouragement, but also realize that the only way you can fight the illness is to first address that the illness exists.

2. Be there

If at all possible, you need to try to be at all the major appointments—especially if your spouse has requested that you be there. Sometimes, it might not make sense, but you still need to do it. Your presence can bring your wife peace. You can be there to physically take care of her, pray with her, hold her hand, console her, and even cry with her if she receives bad test results. Be present to remind your wife that you love her and aren't going to leave her side through this struggle.

3. Lighten the load

When facing a dangerous upcoming surgery or intense treatment, the fear and anxiety that ensues can be overwhelming. No matter which partner is going through the illness, it can affect both. As the healthy spouse, you need to try and bear the load with your spouse as much as possible. When your spouse is having a particularly hard day with pain and anxiety, try to get her out of the house. Sometimes you just need to create a diversion like going to a movie, eating lunch at her favorite restaurant, or taking a walk outside to get some fresh air. It's okay to laugh together. Laughter and smiles are good for the soul. Other times, you just need to listen...to her concerns, fears, details about the surgery or treatment, etc. Whatever you do, your willingness to jump in and lighten the load will help your spouse face this trial without being overtaken by the weight of it all.

4. Honor her requests

In an age of social media, we can let the entire world know about every little detail of our lives with a few clicks on the computer. Social media is a great place to ask for prayers and even needs, but you always need to check with your spouse first. Recently, friends of ours have been facing a debilitating illness, and they have decided to only tell a few friends about it. They did this only because they didn't want too many people showing up at the hospital or making unannounced drop-ins at their house. This may sound harsh to some of you, but I get it. Sometimes we want to put the news out there and accept help and prayers. Other times we just want our inner circle to know. And, that's okay. We have to be sensitive to what our spouse requests during this season.

5. Ask for help

This is especially important when you are going through a long health battle with your spouse. Treatments for diseases, like cancer, can last for months and even years. In order to maintain a job, family life, and some sense of normalcy, you are going to need help. You can't be prideful and decide you can face all these challenges alone. Reach out to friends and family you trust. Sometimes, that means hiring a reliable babysitter, nurse, or cleaning person who can help out during this time. There is no shame in that at all. In fact, the extra hands will allow you to spend more time with your wife.

6. Talk about it

Being there, day in and day out, with a wife who is very ill can certainly take a toll on your own mind and heart. It's important that you have "safe" people in your life with whom you can talk about what you are going through. This person can be a

SAME-GENDER friend, counselor, church leader, or family member (or a brother/sister or parent). He must be someone you can trust with the details of the illness as well as your feelings, plus someone who is encouraging and shares your faith. It's important that this safe person be your same gender to protect you against temptation and inappropriate relationships that could harm your marriage.

7. **Pray about it**

This might be the most important one of all. When you face a serious illness, so much is unknown. All of us need the power of God in our lives. He is our ultimate Healer. He can give us peace that surpasses understanding and a calm in the unpredictable storm. You need to pray together with your wife as well as on your own. Pray for healing, peace, strength, good news, effective medicine, successful surgeries, and support. God hears our prayers and calms our hearts.

More than anything, look at this crisis of illness as an opportunity to honor your marital vow to love each other in both sickness and health. God will use this to strengthen your marriage and your faith if you don't lose hope and if you stay strong together.

Living Out the Sixth Promise: "I Will Love You, in Sickness and in Health."

Of all the vows, the promise to love "in sickness and in health" may be the most challenging because sickness can steal our energy faster than almost anything else. There will be times you can live out this vow in little ways, like pampering your wife with back rubs and chicken noodle soup while she's fighting off a cold. But there may also be times you're called to stand by each other through devastating illness or injury.

If those moments of hardship come, choose to face them together. Make the "ingredients" of a healthy, "naked marriage" a lifelong priority. Take turns being strong for one another in the moments when the other feels weak. Allow your wife to serve you during the times you're not able to take care of yourself—and be willing to do the same for her. Never give up on each other!

PRAYER FOR TODAY

Lord, I pray for Your healing power to protect our family. I know on this side of Heaven our bodies are imperfect. Sickness will come, but even when it comes, help us trust You and lean on each other. Help us use our strength and health to the fullest while we have them. Let us never take for granted a day of health. When illness comes, please prepare our hearts, bodies, and finances to be able to weather the storms. Let us lean on You and each other in those difficult days and look forward to heaven when our bodies will never experience sickness, pain, or death again. Thank You for Your healing power, and thank You for holding us in moments of suffering.

In Jesus' name,
Amen

FOR JOURNALING AND REFLECTION

- What did I learn about my spouse today?
- What did I learn about myself today?

- What did I learn about the promise, "I will love you, in sickness and in health"?
- As a result of what I've learned, I will…

DAY 6 ACTIVITY: GET MOVING

Today's activity is one to get you moving together. Since health has been a theme in this chapter, do something specifically to get your hearts pumping! We love going on long walks as an opportunity to communicate while also getting some exercise and fresh air. Weather permitting, go on a long walk, hike or bike ride together today. Use the time to talk, to enjoy the outdoors, and to get some exercise. If it's raining outside, you can always get some indoor exercise together in the bedroom!

_____
_____
_____
_____
_____
_____
_____
_____
_____
_____
_____
_____
_____
_____
_____
_____
_____
_____
_____
_____

Day 7

UNTIL DEATH DO US PART

———

HEBREWS 12:1-2

Harold and Louise are an extraordinary couple. Ashley and I had the privilege of meeting them at a recent marriage conference we were hosting, and we were instantly drawn to them. There was a sparkle in their eyes and an adoration they obviously had for one another. They couldn't help themselves from smiling every time their eyes met. Even though they were both in their seventies, they acted like two teenagers in love.

We spent as much time around them as we could that weekend because we wanted to learn the "secret" of their lifelong love. I wanted to know how their love had grown richer with time, and how even through painful setbacks in Louise's health, they both remained joyful, optimistic, and passionately devoted to one another.

Louise shared a story with us which gave us a glimpse into their lifelong love. She said, "Our first date was on March 17," she said, "so on April 17, Harold brought me a long-stemmed rose to celebrate our one-month anniversary. I was genuinely impressed by his thoughtfulness, but I didn't expect the roses to come very often. I was so surprised when he brought me another rose on May 17 to celebrate our second month together. I smiled and thought, 'Wow! This fella is a keeper!'"

She smiled at Harold and continued her story. "After we got married, I expected the roses to stop, but on the 17th that first month of our marriage, another rose appeared."

She paused to squeeze Harold's hand, and tears began to form in her eyes as she smiled and said, "It has been fifty-four years since our first date, and every month on the 17th for 648 months in a row, Harold has brought me a rose."

As she finished speaking, I was simultaneously inspired by their love story, and at the same time feeling like an insensitive jerk for never having done anything for Ashley that could match that level of consistent thoughtfulness. Harold definitely challenged me to raise the bar in my own marriage! I obviously can't build a time machine and go back to the beginning and start that type of tradition, but I can bring more thoughtfulness and romance to my marriage, starting today. (You can, too).

Harold and Louise would be quick to tell you it takes a lot more than roses to build a strong, lifelong marriage. The flowers weren't really the point of their story; it was the thoughtfulness behind the flowers. As I spend time with couples who have faithfully loved each other for decades, I'm convinced their "secret" is really no secret at all. It's a simple choice to put love into action by consistently serving, encouraging, supporting and adoring one another.

In this chapter, we're going to explore practical and powerful ways to build the kind of marriage that will remain strong and vibrant through every season of life. We'll start by exploring the power of healthy habits in your marriage.

Developing Healthy Habits in Your Marriage

In his groundbreaking book, *The 7 Habits of Highly Effective People*, Stephen Covey identified the traits which consistently cause people to rise from mediocrity to excellence. The book revealed the timeless truth that our daily habits will be what determine the course of our lives.

This idea might sound revolutionary, but it has been around for a long time. It was the ancient Greek philosopher Aristotle who said, **"We are what we repeatedly do. Excellence, therefore, is not an act, but a habit."**

We have developed a healthy habit of going to the local YMCA. For us, going to the gym is more than just an opportunity to work out. It offers two hours of free childcare—and for parents of three young boys, that's worth its weight in gold! One of our favorite "dates" happens at the Y. While our kids are playing and having fun, we spend the first thirty minutes sitting down, having a cup of coffee, and talking with each other. We make sure the kids know what we're doing, to plant the seed in their young minds that their Mommy and Daddy love each other and make their marriage a priority.

A lot of folks walk in ready for their workout and see us lounging on a loveseat. They sometimes give us funny looks like we're wasting our time. But for us, it's one of the most productive moments of the day. Sure, we might see some benefits from an extra half-hour on the treadmill, but we wouldn't trade that time together for the world. Making time for each other a consistent priority has been one of the most significant, positive decisions we've made for our marriage.

Recently, a guy who works here at the YMCA made a point to stop us and tell us that his daughter and son-in-law were having marriage problems, and he had told them about our little "gym date" routine. He bought them a gym membership and encouraged them to take advantage of the childcare—not only to work out, but to work out their relationship. That was a huge compliment to us and a challenge to continue developing the types of marriage-building habits that are worth imitating. We hope it helps them as much as it has helped us.

Getting your marriage "in shape" isn't all that different from getting your body in shape. You don't get out of shape all at once, and you won't get into shape all at once, but you can make a decision to immediately alter your course in a healthier direction. Over time, those consistent little investments into the health of your relationship will pay huge dividends. Your love handles might not get any smaller, but your love for each will grow—and that's really what counts the most!

8 "Must-Haves" for Your Marriage

Everybody talks about the "must-haves" of the day…the week…the season. Television tells us. Social media shows us. It's up close and in our faces. Usually, these must-haves are just things that will, without a doubt, be replaced by the next hot item of the following season. However, when it comes to marriage, there are certain must-haves that are evergreen.

These are eternal and necessary, and your marriage can't survive without them. Here they are, in no particular order:

1. **Love**

   As we discussed earlier in this devotional, love requires commitment. It's not just a feeling, and it is rooted in truth and transparency. Love is intentional and unconditional. It takes work, just like tending a garden. Love is an action that both partners must choose to do daily.

2. **Respect**

   Have you ever been around a couple who clearly don't respect each other? It's painful to watch and even more painful to live through. How can two people who love and respect each other on their wedding day end up feeling utter disgust toward one another after a few years of marriage? It happens each day we fail to take advantage of the opportunity to show respect to one another. Just like we must choose to love, we must choose to respect each other as well—even on the days when you can't think of anything she has done to gain your admiration. This may seem counter-cultural, but it's so important that you do this for your spouse. Let your wife know you appreciate what she does, but more importantly, tell her you appreciate who she is.

3. Mutual Submission

Submission gets a bad rap, even in the Christian community. However, it is a good thing and God meant for it to be mutual. When both the husband and wife resist being selfish and determine to serve one another, the marriage will thrive. Healthy marital submission occurs when we submit to God first and then to one another. We must humble ourselves and build trust. A marriage cannot survive without trust. Remember: in marriage, we either win together or lose together. When we mutually submit to each other, we surrender our defenses and come together as one. There are certainly specific roles that God assigns to the husband and the wife, but these roles can only be fulfilled properly when both spouses first mutually submit to God and one another.

4. Kindness

This should be a no-brainer, but we know too many married couples who treat each other terribly. This is not only toxic to a marriage and family, but it is simply wrong. Be mindful of your words and treat your spouse kindly every day. Don't fall into the pattern of being kind to every co-worker and perfect stranger you encounter only to come home and verbally throw up or ignore your wife. This is not okay. Harsh words hurt and leave scars. Proverbs 12:25 says, "Anxiety weighs down the heart, but a kind word cheers up the heart." Let's give our kindest words and gestures to our families and cheer them up. Your home should be a place of peace, love, and encouragement, even when you disagree.

5. Daily Communication

Again, this seems like a given, and yet so many couples struggle in this area. We need to communicate—with words—to one another. Put down the phone. Turn off the television. Close the laptop. Give your wife your best attention, not a half-hearted glance from a device. Be willing to put it all away and share your heart with your spouse every day.

6. **Sexual Intimacy**

Sex is important, and God designed it to be a beautiful culmination of love, intimacy, trust, commitment, and pleasure—specifically for a husband and wife. Sex is a good thing, and it should never be abused. We shouldn't use it as a punishment or reward, and we certainly shouldn't withhold it or force it upon one another. The marriage bed should be the safest place on Earth free from judgment, shame, or other sexual partners, whether in person or virtually (i.e. porn). Married couples with the most satisfying sex lives talk openly about their personal desires and lovingly strive to meet each other's needs while keeping their mind and heart fixed on one another.

7. **Non-Sexual Physical Touch**

Physical touch plays a vital role in marriage, but it doesn't always need to lead to sex. A simple hug, pat on the back, kiss, shoulder rub, foot rub, or holding of hands is an intimate gesture of reassurance for the love we feel for one another. Some couples are naturally more affectionate than others, but every couple needs to offer some non-sexual physical touch to one another. Cuddle when you watch television. Hold hands when you go on a walk. Give each other a foot rub. When you willingly serve your wife by engaging in the kind of physical touch that makes her feel loved, you will strengthen your marriage.

8. **Foundation of Faith**

This is the most important one of all. Every marriage will go through rough patches because we are frail human beings who make mistakes. We are all in dire need of a Savior. We thank God every day that He chose to send his Son, Jesus Christ, to be our one and only Savior. He took on all of our sins—even the nastiest, most hateful, disgusting, heart-wrenching, humanly unforgivable ones. He died and paid the price for our sins and rose again so we can live a life of freedom. His love is unfailing, even when our love for one another falls short.

He offers us grace even when we can't find it in our hearts to forgive. When you and your wife have a strong faith in the Lord—both individually and collectively—the foundation for your marriage will be strong. Cover your marriage and family in prayer and know the peace and love only God can provide.

If faith in Jesus is new to you, we encourage you to read the Gospels *(Matthew, Mark, Luke, and John)* in the Bible to learn about Jesus and His tremendous love for you. Becoming a Christian doesn't mean you will be perfect, but it does mean that you will know and be known by a flawless, loving God who has perfect plans for you.

A "Message from God"

As we close the final day's reading, we want to share a story with you that forever changed our perspective about perseverance. I have never heard God audibly speak, but a few years ago, I did receive a "message from God" in a very unlikely way. This simple, two-word message changed my life. I believe it has the power to change your life and your marriage as well.

I had just moved my family to a new city and was serving as a pastor in a new church. The transitions and pressures of life and ministry with a young family were beginning to feel overwhelming. I felt exhausted, misunderstood, frustrated, discouraged, and near the end of my rope. I wanted to quit. For the first time in my adult life, I wanted to do anything but ministry!

I was sharing all of this with my amazing wife one night, and finally, in frustration, I stood up from the couch and began to stomp around the living room like a toddler. I said, "God, it feels like you are being completely quiet right now! Where are you? I could really use a message from you. Just tell me what I'm supposed to do here!"

I plopped back on the couch in frustration and threw my feet up on the coffee table. Ashley looked at my feet and said, "You've got something stuck on your foot." I looked down, and there was a sticker on my heel. It must have been left on the floor by one of my kids. As I peeled it off to look at it, I had to catch my breath because I was overwhelmed by what it said. I was (and still am) convinced that sticker on my foot was as clear a message from God as I have ever received. It simply said, "KEEP GOING!"

That marked a turning point in my attitude and my perspective. I wrote the date "6-30-10" on that sticker and placed it on the front page of my Bible as a constant reminder to "keep going." God gave me the strength to press through that difficult season, and very quickly, almost every area of life and ministry began to improve.

We've all had moments where we've felt like giving up and moments where we've wondered where God was in the midst of it. I pray that you are reminded that God is with you; He is for you; He will carry you through the struggle; He will bring purpose from your pain, and He will reward your faithfulness. Just don't give up. Keep going until you reach the finish line!

In your marriage, you will face great times and tough times, but if you'll hold onto God, hold onto each other and commit to simply "keep going," there is nothing that can stop you or tear you apart!

"...And let us run with endurance the race God has set before us. We do this by keeping our eyes on Jesus, the champion who initiates and perfects our faith." (Hebrews 12:1-2)

Living Out the Seventh Promise: "I Will Love You, Until Death Do Us Part."

Remember that a "perfect marriage" is just two imperfect people who refuse to give up on each other! In every season of your life together, make each other a priority. Be intentional about developing the healthy habits that will set a positive course for your marriage. Keep loving each other, keep encouraging each other, keep praying together, and keep going until God calls you home. Now, get ready for today's activity because the entire experience has been building up to this moment!

PRAYER FOR TODAY

Father, thank You for my wife. Next to Your love, she is the greatest blessing in the world to me. Let me show her my love and commitment in ever-increasing ways through every season of our lives together. Help us keep growing closer to each other instead of drifting apart. Guide us an even more intimate relationship with You and with each other, so that we may cultivate the "naked marriage" You designed the two of us to experience together. Let our love for You and each other create a legacy in our family that will extend for many generations. Let our marriage be a living testimony pointing people to Your goodness and grace. Thank You for the incredible treasure You have given me in my wife.

In Jesus' name,
Amen

FOR JOURNALING AND REFLECTION

- What did I learn about my spouse today?
- What did I learn about myself today?
- What did I learn about the promise, "I will love you, until death do us part"?
- As a result of what I've learned, I will…

DAY 7 ACTIVITY: WRITE AND RENEW

In this final chapter, we want to give you an opportunity to experience a milestone moment with your spouse. It's going to require some thought and preparation on your part, but we promise it will be well worth the effort! We'll begin with the Love Letter Exercise (as we hinted to earlier in the Day 2 activity section) and then lead into a time of renewing your vows. You'll each make a renewed promise of recommitment to each other.

The first step is to take time to write a letter to each other. You can type and print it out if necessary, but I encourage you to write the letter in your own handwriting. Handwritten letters have become so rare in our culture that when we do receive them (especially from a spouse), they are more likely to become a keepsake. Be specific about what you love about your spouse. Make sure it comes from your heart and give it a lot of thought. We believe your spouse will treasure your letter for years to come!

Once you've both written letters, choose a time and place to sit down and take turns reading them. While your wife is reading, let her finish before you respond to her words. End the exercise by sharing your thoughts and feelings with each other and then transition into the renewing of your vows.

_____

_____

_____

_____

_____

_____

_____

_____

_____

_____

_____

_____

_____

_____

_____

_____

_____

_____

_____

_____

_____

_____

_____

_____

_____

_____

_____

_____

_____

_____

_____

_____

_____

_____

_____

_____

_____

_____

Renewing the Vows

Now that you've made it to the end of this journey through the wedding vows, you, hopefully, have a renewed understanding of the six promises that will make or break a marriage. Let's take a moment to recap each one. I'd encourage you to repeat these words to each other as you recommit to your wife and begin a new season of growth in your marriage.

Before you exchange these words, here's a quick recap of what each of these vows really means:

I take you to be my wife…
You are giving the gift of your love to just one person in the entire world. You have chosen your spouse, and they have chosen you! Never lose sight of this beautiful exchange. Be the best husband and wife you can be for one another.

To love and to cherish…
God calls husbands and wives to adore each other and pursue each other with an ever-growing love. This is a commitment to invest in the friendship that sets the foundation for romantic love. This means working

creatively, thoughtfully, and passionately to win the heart of your spouse over and over again.

For better or for worse...
You've got to love each other no matter what. Marital love can't be based on convenience or even feelings. This commitment means that our love will never be dictated by our circumstances. Your vows are most important in the moments when they are least convenient.

In sickness or in health...
You can't always control what happens to your health, but you can control how you choose to respond. Recommit to loving and supporting each other completely in moments of health, but also in moments of injury or illness.

Forsaking all others...
Marriage must remain monogamous. Refuse to allow anyone else to steal your spouse's rightful place in your mind, your heart, or your bed. Recommit to loving each other with wholehearted fidelity and devotion.

For richer or for poorer...
Commit to each other that money will never be your primary pursuit. Your love has nothing to do with whether you're bankrupt or wealthy. Money comes, and money goes, but your commitment to each other must stand firm.

...until death do us part.
These vows are meant to be for a lifetime. Recommit to being there for each other in every season, every struggle, and every set of circumstances. Remember that these vows have no expiration date. Your marriage is a lifelong pursuit and a lifelong commitment.

Once you've had a moment to reflect upon the significance of the vows and the journey you've taken up to this point, please take your spouse's hand and repeat these sacred promises to each other:

"I _____ , take you _____ , to be my wife. To love and to cherish, for better or for worse, for richer or for poorer, in sickness or in health, forsaking all others, 'til death do us part!"

You may now kiss the bride!

Congratulations! You've come to the end of this journey, but it's really more of a starting point than a finish line. We hope this book has helped you refuel your relationship and refocus your resolve as you look to the road ahead. We pray God's continued blessings and guidance for you both through all the celebrations and challenges of life. If you'll continue to walk through life hand-in-hand—trusting God, supporting each other, and striving to "stay naked" physically, mentally, emotionally, and spiritually—there's nothing that can come between you!

ABOUT DAVE & ASHLEY

Dave and Ashley Willis spent thirteen years in full-time church ministry before joining the XO Marriage team to build stronger, Christ-centered marriages. With XO Marriage—the largest marriage-focused ministry in the world—their books, blogs, podcasts, speaking events, and media resources have reached millions of couples worldwide. Dave and Ashley speak at all XO events, host *The Naked Marriage Podcast* and regularly create new marriage resources. They also co-host the MarriageToday broadcast on Daystar Television Network, which features their teachings alongside MarriageToday founder, Pastor Jimmy Evans.

The Willis family includes four sons from preschool to high school age, plus a rescue dog named "Chi-Chi." When Dave and Ashley aren't writing and speaking, they treasure hanging out with their family, watching movies, and taking long walks together to develop new, marriage ministry content ideas.

Follow the Willises on social media:
Facebook: /strongermarriages
Instagram: @daveandashleywillis
and subscribe to their *Naked Marriage Podcast*

ADDITIONAL RESOURCES

MarriageToday Webstore

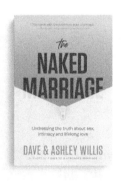

The Naked Marriage: Undressing the Truth About Sex, Intimacy and Lifelong Love
$14.99

The Naked Marriage Discussion Guide: For Couples & Groups
$19.99

Amazon & Other Book Retailers

Raising Boys Who Respect Girls: Upending Locker Room Mentality, Blind Spots, and Unintended Sexism by Dave Willis

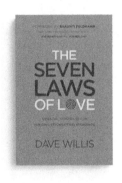

The 7 Laws of Love: Essential Principles for Building Stronger Relationships by Dave Willis

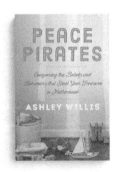

Peace Pirates: Conquering the Beliefs and Behaviors that Steal Your Treasure in Motherhood by Ashley Willis

Made in the USA
Middletown, DE
04 January 2024

47228567R00071